Heart of a Soul Comforter

Kayla Muth

Presentation by *BookLeaf Publishing*

Web: www.bookleafpub.com

E-mail: info@bookleafpub.com

ISBN: 9789395969765

First edition 2022

DEDICATION

For my dad, who kept asking me if I'd written my book yet.

ACKNOWLEDGEMENT

I would like to thank all of the friends and family who encouraged me to write over the years. Your words and belief turned into an internal nagging that I could no longer ignore.

PREFACE

These poems came into being thanks to the overthinking hamster that is constantly running on a wheel inside of my brain. Rather than allow my thoughts to perpetually spin, I ultimately decided to focus. I opted to put pen to paper and found it therapeutic to finally elaborate on my experiences. It is only through a willingness to be vulnerable that we can truly connect in this world, so here are my thoughts laid bare for all to read. So kick back and relax while enjoying the various topics touched upon within these pages.

Vermouth Honesty

Honesty comes with a shot of vermouth
To the cultural elite
And the cop walkin' his beat
All of them equal, like back in their youth

Truth whispers at night to those snorting lines
To the man in the gutter
And the crazies who stutter
It's forceful impact, like exploding mines

Most scientists claim there is no proof
To them, it's all pure folly
Think you've been trippin' on molly
While culture broadcasts, "It's an age old spoof!"

For them, Truth is forever elusive
Refusing to ever hear
Choosing, rather, to cover their ears
Since the evidence is "inconclusive"

But those who hear the knock answer the Truth
Thankfully, they are caving
Admitting they need saving
Honesty comes with a shot of vermouth

Peter & Matthew

Voices.
Voices.
Consumed my existence
Tearing me down with their awful persistence
At night, I could be found curled up in a ball
Convinced I'd amount to nothing at all

Pathetic, I know, to be found like this
Friends would question, "What did I miss?"
"It's anxiety!" I'd say, with a shake of my fist
Unconvinced, they'd often fade like fresh morning
mist

Around then, I was reacquainted with Peter and
Matthew
Who both whispered, "There's someone always
looking out for you;
He cares and desires that you go and seek rest."
But I still thought that I knew what was best

Continually those voices filled me with lies
Seeking to cause my untimely demise
Bombarded with what was considered mainstream
I opted to pursue the American dream
So I chose to put on a mask of piety
In order to hide my crippling anxiety

I spent my days clothed in faux success
But deep down I knew, my life was a mess
The voices were winning, sending me into isolation
Though I refused to give up, if that's any consolation

Again on the road I met up with Peter and Matthew
Who still whispered, "There's someone always
looking out for you;
He cares and desires that you go and seek rest."
But I continued to think I knew what was best

I fought and climbed to that worldly summit
Only to find myself drastically plummet
Anger undermined my pact of nonaggression
I soon found myself spiraling into a deep depression
On occasion, I just wanted to make everything numb
So I turned to my old friend, referred to as rum

But if I'm to be candid
I felt quite stranded
Eventually I reached the end of my rope
And I searched for any grain of hope

So I turned to Peter and Matthew
Who still maintained, "There's someone always
looking out for you;
He cares and desires that you go and seek rest."
I finally knew that I didn't know best

Though I'd fought hard and long
I knew I was going about life all wrong
It was time to put my reliance
In something greater than science
I needed to step back from a dead end profession
Because I felt steered in another direction

Hurricane Sandy rolled through that fall
And I found myself responding to a much different call
With pictures of destruction plastered on the television
I knew serving others was my brand new mission

At my side, I found Peter and Matthew
Who had given me this new point of view
They reminded me to continue to seek rest
And were thrilled when I admitted the One they sought knew what was best

Soon I could be found bagging insulation
Which had to be removed due to storm devastation
Slowly, I worked on dismantling my pride
With brand new friends laboring by my side
I ultimately found rest for my soul
And steadily, I began to feel whole

Presently, you're aware of my greatest sin
Since I've opted to be as transparent as gin
And no longer is my anxiety
Actively killing me silently

So in case you come across Peter and Matthew
Believe them when they say, "There's someone
always looking out for you."
And if they convey for you to go another way
Do yourself a favor and choose to obey
The One who is the only true way

Obedience Hurts

Obedience hurts
It means relinquishing, "I know what's best"
For, "You know what's better."

Obedience means sacrifice
It involves loosening your grip on control
And walking away from your desires.

Obedience requires change
Dreams must be re-routed
Or scrapped entirely.

Obedience isn't giving up
It's redirecting your passions
Following what's important into the unknown.

Obedience demands perseverance
Because it's so easy to rebel
Assuming society has it figured out.

Obedience isn't easy
One must choose the narrow gate
Along the world's wide road.

Obedience saved me from myself
It's taught me to see through lies
And to accept that I'm a misfit.

But that'll never change the fact that
Obedience hurts.

Orange Pants

So many compliments
On my orange pair of pants
People liked my flair and thought I took a chance

Little did they know, that's the true me

I lost years drifting with the status quo
Shuffling through life, day after day
My identity stifled in a color palette of gray

October

In October, I can relate to the roaming gnome
Always traveling, yet never quite whole
Rarely in a place that I can call home
Thankfully, helping others has been good for my soul

In 2013, I ventured to Morehead City
It's a quaint seaside town on everyone's map
Time with friends had me all giddy
Along with this lesson: Don't grow up, it's a trap

2014, I wound up in St. John
Living for a month in island paradise
I hitchhiked around like a true vagabond
And threw a hurricane party where ravioli and rum
sufficed

2015 brought me to Clearlake
Five weeks sifting after a fire
So much stress, I couldn't catch a break
Hopping a flight back east was all I desired

2016, it was on to Baton Rouge
Endless mudouts and lots of tile floors
All thanks to an incredible deluge
I got to see old friends and make plenty more

2017 brought Hurricane Harvey
And I found myself Houston bound
I went from assessing to being team lead
Hardwood floors, tarred to slabs, soon piled in a giant mound

2018 it was on to Jacksonville
Roof after roof, there was so much tarping
The starfish and seven dwarfs used their skills
And thankfully none of us ended up falling

Germany is where I jetted off to in 2019
Visiting friends along the Main and the Rhine
With all of my stress, though, it felt like a bad dream
But I tried to smile through it, telling people, "I'm fine."

Then in 2020, I finally settled in PA
Working at Amazon and dodging coronavirus
Thinking this home is where I might stay
And hoping this election doesn't divide us

In 2021, I remained in PA
Curious about how the year was unfolding
I wandered to Oktoberfest to cheer on dachsunds, eh
Helping strangers place bets before some stein holding

Now in 2022, it's back to Germany
Almost as if on cue
Time to make memories with friends and family
Especially my swiftly growing nephew

Off to Brooklyn

Vagabond alone
Ponder your life
Meet lots of people
Have a good laugh

Feel disconnected
Miss your friends
Traveling your life's
Peculiar path

Alone again
Sitting in a booth
This seems to be a trend
A rather uncomfortable truth

Young Jack Kerouac
Would idealize travel
It's true connection I lack
Remaining stoic, my mind won't unravel

This Comfort Inn
My temporary home
Tomorrow, I'm off to Brooklyn
As I continue to perpetually roam

This is what you'll find
I'm always miles away
But will I cross someone's mind
Even though I refuse to ever stay?

Insatiable Wanderlust

Years spent on the road
Various landscapes trickling from view
Helping others after disasters
It's what I felt called to do

Oddly at peace within these walls
Resting in my tiny six by eight
The Holy Spirit being the cause
Whoever knew this would be my fate?

We come to serve
And end up blessed
Reminded the presence of Jesus
Provides true rest

Bonds were formed with volunteers
And even some homeowners, too
But then we'd disperse back to our homes
Except, I had no home to venture back to

I feel like I'm always leaving, never staying
And that truly breaks my heart
There's a revolving door of people in my life
The ones I truly love, we're always miles apart

Just a Phase

You're half a world away
Yet still cross my mind
I'm here wondering if you're okay
But that answer is always hard to find.

My wandering has cost me
Community. Intimacy. A sense of belonging.
COVID-19 finally made me see
Family. Friendships. For this I've been longing.

But you knew all this, way back when
I sat across from your penetrating gaze
Attempting to dodge your questions and then
Slowly accepting that vagabonding is just a phase.

Fluctuating Emotions

So easily people forget
That it is written, "Jesus wept."

How long must Christians in duress
Be told their emotions, they must suppress?

Dreams shatter like an ornament on the floor
If life continues this way, I can't take much more

My look is reflexive conveying disdain
Eyes flickering in anger, an impatient spark

The darkness inside has seeped to the surface
Now being around me makes others quite nervous

Hopelessly waiting, unwelcome thoughts keep
invading
The way my brain functions is a blessing and a curse

Anxiety haunting me
My mind can't rest, wish I could be free

Cortisol flows out of sight
Thoughts are racing, always fight or flight

Resting heart rate ninety-six
Is this something only God can fix?

Understanding hard to find
People perplexed, just silence your mind

Running hamster, use a wedge
To stop the wheel, always on edge

Listening to you talk created these cracks in me
Too many stories and half truths
Now make me unsure of what I can believe

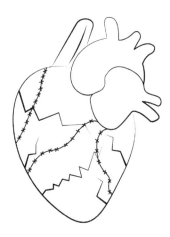

Resentment & Forgiveness

Pedestals shatter
Under the weight of expectations
Our desire to raise others up
Only leads to devastation

Resentment chokes the life out of love
Its roots are made of bitterness and envy
Eliminating it requires drastic measures
For the sake of your relationships, rise above

How swiftly we throw others under the bus
It's a knee-jerk reaction as our fear grows
Even Peter denied Jesus before three cock crows
Yet the Gospel still demands we grant forgiveness

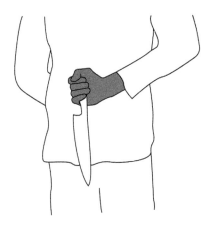

Jesus & Judas

Jesus still washed Judas' feet
Knowing full well his heart was full of deceit
Knowing his kiss would betray the next time
they'd meet
Knowing He'd be taken by soldiers to be beat
Knowing He'd face death, but not defeat
Jesus still washed Judas' feet

Rat Race Investments

Investing demands risk
Fiscally and relationally
It requires fortitude of both heart and mind

Brokenness makes us all hypervigilant
Those near us question our sincerity
Yet folks desire to be seen candidly

The rat race says, "Give up on society."
Dodge every insipid individual
And move on when we're ultimately stonewalled

Rather than admit defeat, choose to dig in
Ask deep questions and insist on their answers
Facades crumble and people want to be known

So shelve anxiety
Dismantle your walls, opt to reach out
And let people know they are appreciated

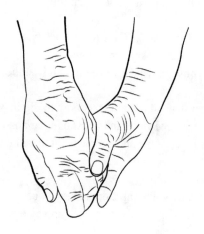

Life Happens

Life happens in-between social media posts
It's not all sunsets, concerts, and travel
Rather it happens during mundane tasks
And if you're truly blessed, someone will invite you
in

It happens when a friend cleans out Grandma's
freezer
Or during court appointed classes
It happens in the car after work
Or in hospital waiting rooms

It happens after failed sporting events
Or after the passing of a cat
It happens when chiseling a car out of a snowbank
Or curled up on the cold bathroom floor

It happens when teaching backgammon at
Thanksgiving
Or fixing E20 codes on washers
It happens during produce auctions
Or during games of memory

It happens when shopping for a funeral dress
Or when doctors don't have answers
It happens after sprained ankles
Or during impromptu flights to Atlanta

And it happens in crowded grocery stores
When the task of shopping is too overwhelming
These moments are what truly make up life
And should be cherished at all costs

Words of Significance

Underlining obsessively
These books are marred
By my desire to remember quotes and imagery

Words are sapped of significance
Lacking impact
I yearn to reestablish them to their former glory

So I will write to share my thoughts
Show that I care
While ironically rejecting any written to me

Understanding aggressively
This connection
Between accepted and rejected remarks can weary

Words can stick like gorilla glue
Having impact
They cripple or invigorate, often hard to carry

So decide what you're permitting
Soul comforter
A profound description that a friend once gifted to
me

Gray Elephants

I'm writing you this day
On behalf of these elephants
To remind you the color gray
Is not completely irrelevant

Now don't get discouraged
Always thinking in black and white
Deep within, you have much courage
Rising each day to put up a fight

So silence the voices
Don't let them steal your potential
You've got to sift through life's choices
Always remembering you're special

Gypsy Possum

There once was a gypsy possum
Who thought that camels were awesome
Soon a lemming agreed
Saying they were cool indeed
Now just watch their friendship blossom

Reminiscence

Symphony Number 5 plays in the background
As I try to gather my thoughts
It's amazing what music brings to mind
Sometimes memories long forgot

This classic brings me back to childhood
And the time spent with my brother
Bugs Bunny was a constant
Presenting new overtures for us to discover

Animals, too, jolt my brain back in time
Horses, a chuckle they'll elicit
In Illinois, they taunted an innocent party
We made our instructions quite explicit

Pool tables conjure specific locations
A friend's basement and the Cinder Inn, I recall
There's also a Texas honky tonk
And Puerto Rico, where I scratched on the 8 ball

Weddings bring forth joy and laughter
But not for the reasons you're thinking
I just remember wandering into a church
Searching for a bathroom after all the water
we'd been drinking

Memories are planted and then they grow
Only God knows their specific reason
Thankfully, they can be swiftly retrieved
To bring forth a smile during difficult seasons

For now, autumn sun peaks through the clouds
As my mind drifts back to spring
That's when we encountered bustling crowds
In search of glasses of Riesling

Effervescence

You need friends in your life who embody
effervescence
People who exude joy while getting you a shirt off a
store mannequin
Those who remind you to drink your sunshine juice
in the morning and get excited about MREs

Friends who are enthusiastic about exploring a hotel
for hours or shopping at a foreign grocery store
People who will write encouraging notes and take
you on beach camping trips
Those who determine they wanna be your best friend
even though your first thought is, "Can I trust them?"

Friends who don't judge you for breakfast beers and
chocolate on early morning trains
People who are mesmerized by empty cathedrals in
sleepy towns
Those who encourage your love of maps and
icecream

Friends who don't question wandering back to town
for a bottle of Starling Castle, all just to make change
for train tickets
People who love sailing as much as you do and
happen to play street pianos

And especially those willing to stand by you when world governments and media outlets opt to vilify you based on personal decisions

Friends like this remind you of the underlying vibrancy life has to offer and help eliminate the darkness that tries to destroy you from within People who add zest to your life just by existing, Those are the ones you should keep by your side.

Long Island Sound

Foghorn in the mist
Ripples fan out from shore
A boat, Ramona

Battle on the Pitch (An Ode to Soccer)

They dress in pressed uniforms and lace up polished
boots
Hair styled to make a statement
Hoping to fuel propaganda
Evaluating many years of training
Sweat trickles down their brows
Lined up in formation, they march down the tunnel

Emerging onto the battle pitch
Enemies absorb their surroundings
Trumpets blare, voices thunder
Opposing forces waving flags
Tempers flare on painted faces
Listen to their violent cries

Stoic they stand while the anthems of nations play
Anxiously they wait to enter into combat
In the distance
Over the cacophony
They finally hear the whistle

The ground shakes
Opponents clash
The captain yells out orders
Attackers dive
Defenders lose ground
One side is heading to the slaughter

Battles rage on, day after day
Blood is spilled
Players ejected
Most dreams end in failure
Few move on, for the next round is reserved
For those who did not falter

Riots erupt, fueled by devoted followers
Refusing to accept defeat
Each day, a new hero is crowned
Worshipped across a nation
And in his hometown

At the culmination of a tumultuous month
The last victor stands triumphant
Hoisting the golden statue in the air--the symbol of a
champion
That's the beauty of the World Cup

New Year

Here I sit on the eve of a new year
With my thoughts drifting to those who are no longer
here
Eight souls God determined to call home
Leading them to rest in eternal shalom

So don't judge my lack of holiday cheer
While I sit alone with my cold beer
You have loved ones that you can go hug
My warmth comes from the splash of bourbon in my
mug

But still, I'm grateful for the memories etched in my
mind
Because they remind me how our lives intertwined
As Mumford sings of ghosts flickering from view
I cling to some hope in the darkness as I bid this year
a weary adieu

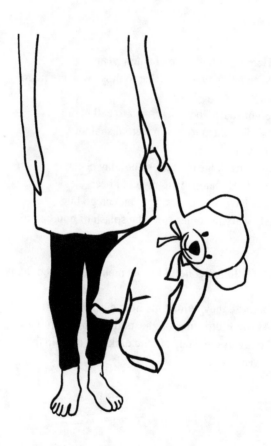

Printed in the USA
CPSIA information can be obtained
at www.ICGtesting.com
LVHW010926101123
763485LV00091B/3904

9 789395 969765